# A Positive Penalty

# The Report of an Inspection of Community Service Placements in Aberdeenshire, Dundee and Falkirk

SOCIAL WORK SERVICES INSPECTORATE FOR SCOTLAND

1997

# Purpose and responsibilities

Our purpose is to work with others to continually improve social work services so that:

- they genuinely meet people's needs; and

- the public has confidence in them.

Member of
Plain English Campaign
committed to
clearer communication

PEC

The Social Work Services Inspectorate
James Craig Walk
Edinburgh
EH1 3BA

# Foreword

This report presents findings and recommendations from our inspection of Community Service placements in Aberdeenshire, Dundee and Falkirk. The three areas inspected offered every co-operation to the inspection team and I am grateful to them.

We found much good practice. The work of Community Service benefits the community and is valued by recipients. We were impressed with the supervisors employed by the Community Service schemes and those working in the voluntary organisations that hosted placements.

There are areas for improvement. The induction process should be more comprehensive and ensure offenders understand the reparative nature of Community Service. The potential for community service to contribute to the reduction of further offending needs to be exploited and more attention given to the contribution the order can make to changing behaviour and attitudes. The requirement for those undertaking Community Service to wear marked clothing should be reviewed.

ANGUS SKINNER
Chief Inspector of Social Work Services for Scotland

# CONTENTS

## Chapter 1

# Introduction

### What are Community Service Orders?

1.    The Community Service Order (CSO) was introduced in Scotland as a sentence of the court in 1979. Under the Criminal Procedure (Scotland) Act 1995 it is an alternative to a custodial sentence. Local authorities provide Community Service schemes as part of their statutory responsibility for criminal justice social work services. Central government, as part of its 100% funding arrangements for these services, bears the full cost and their operation is regulated by National Objectives and Standards. In 1994 (the latest year for which figures are available, 4,270 offenders were sentenced to CS and a further 1,022 were ordered to do CS as part of their Probation Order. A total of 622,966 hours of unpaid work was ordered by the courts.

2.    Offenders undertake a given number of hours of unpaid work, ranging from 80 hours (in all courts) to 240 hours in summary proceedings and 300 hours in solemn court proceedings. They must complete the order within 12 months of the date of the order. The supervising officer of the local authority should "take reasonable steps to enable the offender to complete his/her order" and to enforce that order.

3.    Offenders must report to their supervisor when required, and tell him or her of any change in employment or change of address. They must be punctual and must work to a satisfactory standard. If they fail to keep any of the requirements of the order, they are liable to disciplinary action and they may be returned to court to decide whether they are in breach of the order. Where an offender breaches the order, the court may impose a fine and allow the order to continue or may vary the number of hours. The court may also revoke the order and replace it with another sentence, which can include imprisonment.

### Research on CS outcomes

4.    Research by McIvor (1992)[1] suggests that CS can make a contribution to reducing offending where offenders view the work as "worthwhile". The characteristics identified by McIvor of a "worthwhile" placement are:-

•    placements that maximise contact between offenders and recipients;

•    work that allows the offenders to develop new skills;

•    work that offenders see as benefiting the community.

The relationship with the supervisor was found to be important with an emphasis placed on offenders being treated with dignity and fairness.

---

[1] McIvor, G(1992), Sentenced to Serve, Aldershot: Avebury.

## National standards

5.    National Objectives and Standards state that 'Community Service schemes should be characterised by:

- 'partnership with local communities in the provision of work opportunities and placement agencies;

- a range of agencies offering placements that are of value to the community, the agency and the offender alike;

- a range of placements within the capacity of the offender and capable of enhancing his/her social responsibility and self respect;

- a sufficient range of placements, suited to the particular needs and requirements of groups such as women (including those who are pregnant), people who are disabled and single parents;

- clear, realistic, but challenging standards of behaviour and work.'

Community Service placements should be safe and expected standards of conduct stated clearly to offenders.

6.    Where offenders are on placements with other agencies, Community Service staff must consider carefully the suitability of the placement. They must ensure that the host organisation has enough information about each offender to be able to manage the placement and that they receive proper support and prompt action where necessary from the social work department. The host agency should be fully aware of the standards of behaviour expected from those undertaking Community Service.

## Circular No: SWSG 12/96 - Community Service by Offenders: Public Awareness, Environmental Work and Hours.

8.    The Scottish Office issued a circular on 24 April 1996 (SWSG 12/96) which gives further guidance on community service placements. CS should be 'suitably rigorous and challenging'; 'involve the offender both in making reparation and in contributing to the local community' and be viewed by both the offender and the community as constructive. The circular seeks a greater emphasis on 'physically demanding placements' and requests local authorities to give particular attention to developing environmental improvement projects.

## Realistic and Rigorous

9.    In 1996 The Social Work Services Inspectorate (SWSI) completed an inspection 'Realistic and Rigorous' on the discipline and enforcement of CSOs in two local authority areas. The focus of that inspection was enforcement practices and adherence to the requirements of National Standards. The inspection noted satisfactory practice in one authority but poor practice in some teams in another authority. The report 'Realistic and Rigorous' made a number of recommendations to speed up breach proceedings, strengthen

enforcement processes and improve systems to ensure compliance with standards. The report did not cover placements or the role of the placement supervisor

10.   This inspection report builds on 'Realistic and Rigorous'. It examines the contribution work placements and supervisors make to the management of and compliance with CSOs. It also examines whether the work demands on CS placements are challenging for offenders and credible with the courts.

**This Inspection**

11.   This inspection sought to investigate the current level of placement quality in three local authorities. We sought to identify the ways in which the quality of work placements might be improved and contribute to successful completion and the reduction of re-offending. Drawing on evidence from a range of different sources (sentencer and government expectations, research, statistics and National Standards) we identified a series of questions for investigation.

- Are the work placements credible and challenging?

- Are sheriffs confident about the placements provided in their area?

- Do the placements make real demands on offenders?

- Does the range of placements match the capacities of offenders?

- Do they protect the Health and Safety of all concerned?

- Do the placements benefit the community and do offenders think that the work they are undertaking is of value?

- Do the schemes provide a wide enough range of placements to cater for offenders with different abilities and characteristics?

- Is the treatment of offenders firm and fair?

- Are the placements effective? Do placements and the supervision of the work contribute to successful completion of orders and contribute to reduced risk of re-offending?

**Methods**

12.   The authorities inspected were **Dundee, Aberdeenshire and Falkirk**. In each area:-

- we sought the views of sheriffs, and recipients of CS by way of a questionnaire survey;

- we observed task group and individual placements and interviewed recipients and offenders on the placements;

- we interviewed CS staff and managers;

- we examined a sample of social work case files (breach, successful completion and where the offenders were assessed as unsuitable for CS by social work staff);

- we analysed reports from each area about the range, nature and content of the placement projects;

- we analysed statistics about the number of orders, successful completion, breach, nature and type of placements and range of recipients receiving help from CS;

All three areas provided more information as the inspection progressed to highlight areas of practice.

13.   The inspection has been hampered by insufficient, up to date information on CS outcomes from the National Core Data System.

**The Inspection team**

14.   Inspection Manager - Felim O'Leary (SWSI Assistant Chief Inspector)

Lead Inspector - Stella Perrott (SWSI Inspector)

Administrator - John Williamson (SWSI Administrator)

## Chapter 2

# Placement profiles

**Dundee**

1.    **Dundee** City is an urban area with a narrow rural hinterland serving a population of 153,710. It has high levels of unemployment (10.7%) and some parts of the city have been identified as having particularly high levels of deprivation. The sample of CS files we inspected showed that the majority of offenders had unstable family histories, chronic ill health, lack of social skills and high levels of drug/alcohol dependency.

2.    **Dundee** City Council restructured the CS scheme in **Dundee** in September 1996. The changes relate to the management and organisation of the work rather than the nature of the CS placements although in any period of change the effects will go beyond the immediate focus for change.

3.    CS is managed by a senior social worker. There are 6 social workers in the team (who also supervise some probation cases and prepare a number of SERs), a workshop supervisor and 6 task group supervisors.

4.    In 1994, 203 offenders were placed on CS and 28,734 hours unpaid work was ordered by the courts. In the same year 72 (70%) completed their orders successfully. Thirty-three (30%) orders were breached and terminated. For consistency across all three areas, we have used the 1994 figures from the National Core Data System. More recent figures provided by **Dundee** show a significant increase in the number of orders (24%) and hours over the past three years.

| | |
|---|---|
| 1993-1994 | 225 orders |
| 1994-1995 | 230 orders |
| 1995-1996 | 249 orders |
| 1996-1997 | 280 orders (projected figure) |

| Group placements | |
|---|---|
| *Tasks* | *Recipients* |
| *General work e.g. clearing leaves* | *Zoo* |
| *Gardening* *Painting and decorating* | *Individuals and community groups e.g. community centres* |
| *Workshop - making toys, fencing, and furniture* | *Local charities, wider community* |
| *Environmental* | *Local communities, zoo, visitors to the area.* |

5

| Individual placements | |
|---|---|
| Tasks | Recipients |
| General work e.g. cleaning | Charity Shops |
| Special needs care | Individuals and community groups (mental/physical disabilities) |
| Personal care | Individuals and community groups working for those disadvantaged e.g. homeless and young people |

5.    Many projects have been in existence for a number of years, for example, work at a zoo. Other projects such as work with homeless people and Victim Support have been developed within the past twelve months.  Generally placements were triggered by the recipient through local networks.

### Aberdeenshire

6.    **Aberdeenshire** is a mainly rural area with a population of 223,630 in small scattered communities. Public transport is limited. Employment prospects are good but most of the employment undertaken by offenders is contractual and short term (for example fish packing).  Although there is a significant amount of drug taking, it is not a chronic problem. Most of offenders come from reasonably stable families and enjoy good health. A number of offenders on CS had learning difficulties.

7.    Following local government re-organisation, **Aberdeenshire** organises and manages the CS scheme in the Northern part of the authority.  Aberdeen City manages the scheme in the South but are about to transfer it to **Aberdeenshire**.  For inspection purposes, we looked only at those projects located in the North because they are organised and managed solely by **Aberdeenshire.**

8.    The CS scheme in the North undertakes work in three main areas - Fraserburgh, Peterhead and Banff. CS is only one aspect of wider criminal justice duties for both the senior social worker based at Banff and 2 social workers in each of the 3 areas. There is a full time CS supervisor based at Banff and 0.7 of a supervisor based at Peterhead.

9.    In 1994 (and covering the whole of **Aberdeenshire**) 125 offenders were placed on CS and 18,491 hours of unpaid work was ordered.  In the same year 49 (87%) completed their orders successfully. Eight (13%) orders were breached and terminated. The number of CSOs has been consistent over the past few years and the projected number for all of Aberdeenshire for 1996-1997 is 125.

10.    The main employment in North Aberdeenshire is fishing and oil. As neither of these industries have regular work hours, it is difficult to predict when those with jobs will be available for CS work and those in employment generally undertake CS on a Sunday. There are also arrangements for offenders to report for CS as and when they are on shore during the week.

| **Group Placements** | |
|---|---|
| *Tasks* | *Recipients* |
| *General work e.g. cleaning, gardening.* | *Community groups, homes for the elderly.* |
| *Painting and decorating.* | *Individuals and community groups e.g. community centres.* |
| *Workshop - making toys, fences etc.* | *Local charities.* |

| **Individual Placements** | |
|---|---|
| *Tasks* | *Recipients* |
| *General work.* | *Charity shop, church hall, luncheon and youth clubs.* |
| *Care assistance.* | *Home for the elderly, special needs/children, young people.* |
| *Special needs.* | *Children through community group.* |

11.   Due to the small numbers of offenders on CS at any one location, the opportunities for working in groups of any size is limited and a large percentage of offenders are on individual placements. The placements that are suitable for team working (for example manual help) are undertaken by a group if there are enough offenders available but will otherwise be undertaken by an individual. Most of the work undertaken by offenders on CS is manual. CS have some care tasks for the elderly and there is one project working directly with people with learning difficulties but this was not operating at the time of the inspection.

## Falkirk

12.   **Falkirk** is an urban area with a substantial rural hinterland and a population of 142,000.  Employment in the area is above the national average. Case files indicated that there is some ill health but it is not chronic. There is a significant amount of drug/alcohol abuse.  In comparison with offenders in more deprived urban areas, offenders on CS tend to be in reasonable health, with fewer dependency problems and from reasonably stable families.

13.   In 1994, 157 offenders were placed on CS and 26,060 hours of unpaid work was ordered by the courts. In the same year 76 (64%) completed their orders successfully. Thirty-eight (34%) orders were breached and terminated.  The current figures provided by **Falkirk** show that the number of CSOs has fluctuated in the past three years.

|  |  |
|---|---|
| 1993-1994 | 134 orders |
| 1994-1995 | 161 orders |
| 1995-1996 | 137 orders |
| 1996-1997 | 150 orders (projected) |

14.   A senior social worker manages the dedicated CS team.  There are  2 CS officers (and one vacancy at the time of the inspection) and three full time supervisors.

| Group Placements | |
| --- | --- |
| *Tasks* | *Recipients* |
| *General work, gardening.* | *Community groups, homes for the elderly.* |
| *Painting and decorating.* | *Individuals and community groups e.g. sports clubs.* |
| *Environmental.* | *Wider community.* |

| Individual Placements | |
| --- | --- |
| *Task* | *Recipient* |
| *General work.* | *Charity shop, church hall, luncheon and youth clubs.* |
| *Special needs.* | *Children through community group.* |
| *Literacy and numeracy.* | *Community education project.* |

15.   Projects at the time of the inspection, were mainly environmental and  of a manual nature.  There were some projects that offered assistance with personal care/education for a number of client groups such as young people, the elderly and people with learning difficulties.  We were told that, at the time of the inspection, the emphasis on outdoor manual work over the winter was unusual and that generally there were more painting and decorating projects.  Since the field work, more painting and decorating work is planned alongside some work for people with physical disabilities.  There is considerably more work group than individual placements.

# Chapter 3
# Credible and challenging

**Views of Sheriffs**

1. We sought the views of 7 sheriffs and all responded. All said that punishment, reparation, re-integration of offenders in the community and prevention of further offending were all important sentencing objectives when sentencing to CS. They made very little distinction between the degree of importance given to each objective: if anything they thought re-integration of the offender and prevention of offending were slightly more important than punishment or reparation.

2. They also thought that CS had an important role in reducing re-offending through

- developing work discipline and skills

- encouraging acceptance of responsibility and increasing self respect

One commented for example- 'To educate offenders as to the need to accept responsibility for their own actions, giving of regular attendance and satisfactory performance; to open their eyes to what, with some effort on their part, they can achieve; to encourage them to develop newly developed skills which may lead them in to training or employment and thus reduce the risk of re-offending'.

3. In discussing the ways in which CS could be challenging for offenders, sheriffs mentioned 'hard work', the development of 'self discipline' and the importance of 'motivation', 'self esteem' and 'being positive'. One said for example CS should 'try to introduce some discipline into sometimes chaotic lifestyles, to pay back the community for the offences they have committed, and hopefully allow them to gain self esteem from helping others'.

4. All stated that they would like to use CS for offenders other than those who might be at risk of a custodial sentence. There are indications that some may already be doing so.

**Dundee**

5. All of the sheriffs in **Dundee** (3) indicated that they had confidence in the CS scheme and held it in high regard. Contact between sheriffs and social work services was good and sheriffs were knowledgeable about the work of CS. Sheriffs indicated that drug abusers, those with health problems and those with histories of failure to complete orders may be unsuitable for CS. The file inspection suggested that although CS staff sometimes stated that these offenders were unsuitable in their court reports, CS was ordered none the less, and many completed their orders satisfactorily. **Dundee** have developed a 'light duties' task group where less physically robust offenders can undertake less physically demanding

work. This may meet the request of one sheriff who hoped that more "menial" work might mean a wider range of offenders such as drug addicts could undertake CS.

6.    The scheme in **Dundee** caters for a wide range of offenders. The offenders on CS appeared to be predominantly young, of high risk of re-offending, and are sometimes difficult to manage. They were often suffering ill health or disability, with severe alcohol/drug dependency problems in many cases. There were suitable placements for those with health problems, responsibilities for dependants or those with poor physical, mental or social abilities. There was a sufficient range of suitable placements to ensure work for almost any offender if the court wished to impose a CSO.

## Aberdeenshire

7.    Both sheriffs responded to the questionnaire. One indicated that he knew about the range and nature of CS placements from frequent discussions with social workers. However he appeared to initiate these discussions and suggested that 'consultation with the sentencer may also be helpful'. Both thought the scheme offered benefits to the community but one stated that the 'type of work is unduly restricted. More public projects and recognition would make the concept more attractive to the community'. The end of sentence reports were mentioned by one sheriff as a particularly positive aspect of the scheme and he was satisfied with the scheme.

8.    Due to the rural nature of **Aberdeenshire** with dispersed populations, there were a number of individual placements with community organisations. The work patterns of many offenders pose considerable logistical problems and a flexible, pragmatic approach to CS work patterns is needed. The offenders on CS appeared to be (in comparison with those living in deprived urban areas) in good health, often in employment, with good social skills and without chronic dependency problems. Information contained in the files did not suggest that the nature of the projects available precluded any offenders from CS and most of the offenders on whom the courts wished to impose CS could be placed.

## Falkirk

9.    Both Sheriffs responded to the questionnaire. One said that his knowledge of the scheme was good from contact with social workers and completion reports. Whilst he was happy with the scheme and considered CS a positive sentence he felt that it was too restrictive in terms of both the work undertaken and the narrow group for whom it is considered suitable. The second sheriff said that he did not know about the range of CS placements. We looked at a sample of recent SERs where the report writer assessed the offender as unsuitable for CS. We found that, in many cases, only manual work in a task group was available. For those offenders who were unsuitable for this work, no other work was offered to the offender or the court. **Falkirk Council should increase its range of placements in consultation with the sheriffs so that those offenders the courts might wish to sentence to CS can be placed.**

10.   Offenders who are not suitable for group placements because of the nature of their offence (for example sex offenders) may have an individual placement. Those who have particular relevant skills might also have an individual placement. Individual placements are not however generally available as a different challenge to manual work or as a

placement option in their own right. One offender, who CS staff considered to be unsuitable because of health problems (but was none the less given an order), was sentenced to CS in September 1996. She was still unplaced at the time of the inspection (mid January 1997) and this is unacceptable. We are not confident that the CS scheme in Falkirk provides the range and nature of placements to ensure that all those the courts wish to sentence can be placed properly and quickly. **Arrangements and suitable projects should be in place to ensure that all offenders placed on CS are working within 21 days of sentence as required by National Standards.**

## The public and beneficiaries

11.   The circular 'Community Service by Offenders: Public Awareness, Environmental Work and Hours' reinforces the need for projects to be credible with the public and CS to be seen to be contributing to the local community.   Whilst it was beyond the scope of the inspection team to canvass the views of the public at large, we did seek the views of those who benefit from the work done by offenders on CS since they too are members of the public and many represent community groups such as elderly people. A total of 43 beneficiaries responded to the questionnaire of which 27 were community organisations. We asked beneficiaries about the range of work they thought CS should undertake.  They suggested a wide range of work, mainly helping elderly or disabled individuals.  Only 2 beneficiaries mentioned projects that benefited  the wider community such as removing graffiti  or environmental work.  They also expected a high standard of work and behaviour while appreciating that offenders had varying skills and abilities.

12.   Almost all the beneficiaries spoke highly of the offenders they met and four explicitly stated that the contact they had with the offenders was positive.   It was also clear from other comments that many valued the contact with offenders in a safe environment and seemed to welcome the opportunity to relate to them as people rather than 'offenders'. Such contact may allow the 'public' a more positive experience of offenders and crime, and assist re-integration of offenders into the community.

13.   Both **Dundee** and **Falkirk** had projects that were very visible and of clear benefit to local communities: for example, the clearing of graffiti on a row of shops in **Dundee** and path clearing in Bo'ness for residents from a local estate.  In both cases the local community was aware of who was doing the work.  The comments of some passers by suggested that they appreciated the work. However one project team had to face the disappointment of their work being spoilt by the re-appearance of graffiti overnight. Another  had to cope with harassment by local youths.

14.   Offenders knew very little about CS prior to sentence. Most public awareness of CS comes through word of mouth and recommendations.  Elderly people in a neighbourhood talk to others about work that CS has done for them and this leads to further requests. Referrals by local councillors are an important source of work, particularly in respect of environmental projects or assistance to vulnerable people who need help and councillors pass on their knowledge about the CS scheme.

**Physical demands**

15.   If 'demanding' is defined as 'hard physical labour', then the work we saw on the inspection cannot be described as such and that was also the view of offenders. However the work required sustained effort over a long period by people who are unused to a working routine and who did not feed themselves properly. In winter outdoor work can be especially demanding.

16.   From the offenders' perspective the most challenging aspects of CS were

- the restrictions imposed on their liberty;

- working for nothing;

- having to get up in the morning, get to work, do what they are told and co-operate with others;

- periods of inactivity (for example quiet periods in a charity shop or waiting for painting materials on site), and in some cases

- difficulty in achieving the standard of work required.

Although some offenders (usually those on agency placements) were committed to the work they were doing, the majority wished only to complete their hours. Their experience of CS did not challenge them to confront the reasons for the CSO or how each work session was an opportunity to 'pay back' for harm caused. It was merely a sentence of the court that they had to comply with.

17.   **We were concerned about lost time at the beginning of the working day** (losses of **Dundee** 30 minutes and **Falkirk** 1 hour were observed) because of late arrivals and the preparatory work required before starting work. In **Dundee** work preparations were hampered by the workshop layout and this is now being addressed. In **Aberdeenshire** most of the offenders were picked up in crew buses and so there was little waiting time but considerable travelling time prior to the start of the day.  Whilst it is not necessary to pick offenders up in many of the areas, including rural **Aberdeenshire,** the cost of bus fares in some cases is prohibitive for the offender or the local authority.

18.   The more effort expended the greater the satisfaction. Physically demanding projects were seen as 'satisfying' by the offenders and they enjoyed the physical activity, regardless of their skills and abilities.  In **Dundee** it was sometimes difficult to 'move on' offenders to projects that might be more personally challenging and offer greater benefit to the community. The offenders began to enjoy the work they were doing and the experience of working in a 'team'.

**Social and Emotional Demands**

19.   For those offenders on agency placements, the work often involved close contact with the elderly, people with learning difficulties or a physical disability.  The work required patience, understanding of the needs of others and sensitivity.  For those who were able to cope with the demands of the task it became a rewarding and enjoyable experience.  In

many of these placements, the offenders had to overcome their own fears and misapprehensions about the individuals they were helping. This was challenging for them.

## Skills Demands

20.   Comments from supervisors, recipients and offenders all indicate that the majority of offenders worked hard whilst on placement. They worked close to the limits of their skills and competence but not beyond them. Supervisors were aware that the challenge for offenders and themselves lay in getting that balance right and they were acutely aware of how important that part of their task was. Given the low level of competence of some of the offenders, supervisors sometimes needed to 'hold back' offenders who were too energetic as accidents might otherwise occur or the quality of the work would suffer.

21.   To ensure that CS is challenging for all offenders there needs to be a wide range of projects demanding different levels of skill. There also needs to be opportunities for placements to become more demanding once offenders have learned the basic skills and work habits. Many of the offenders have few work skills to offer and are in poor physical and/or mental health. It will be the most able, the most socially skilled and the healthiest offenders who will be least challenged by CS.

22.   In **Dundee** there was a wide range of projects demanding different levels and types of skills. Offenders who were lacking basic skills could work in well supervised task groups and progress to individual placements. In **Aberdeenshire** the logistics of managing offenders whose days off were unpredictable, meant that matching depended on who was available to meet work commitments rather than the type of work that would challenge the offender. Additionally, a number of older offenders had work skills and had held down jobs for considerable periods of time. For them the challenge was the loss of leisure time and the length of time it took them to complete their order. The projects available in **Falkirk** limited skills development to a basic level. Unless the offender had an agency placement, there were few opportunities to progress or meet greater challenges through more complex work. The supervisors did try and vary the tasks on the work group to take account of the different abilities and to seek opportunities to stretch offenders' capabilities. **Falkirk should ensure that there are sufficient projects available so that offenders use a wider range of skills and that placements are sufficiently challenging.**

# Chapter 4

# **Appropriate and Achievable**

1.    In all areas assessment of CS suitability and allocation to projects includes consideration of the current offence, offending history, health and social circumstances. In **Dundee** the assessment is thorough and placement matching is according to social and work skills, interests and degree of supervision required. In **Aberdeenshire** the type of work project greatly depends on offender availability and there is limited matching for suitability. In **Falkirk** staff generally assume that all offenders will go to task groups where work is physically demanding. Where this is not a realistic option, an alternative placement will be considered but offenders considered to be unsuitable for task group placements are frequently viewed as unsuitable for CS.

2.    Beneficiaries indicated that

- most of the offenders on CS were suitably skilled for the work;

- they were able to meet the required standards of work;

- the standard of work achieved by the offenders was high;

- behaviour was good;

- the offenders put effort into the tasks;

- they were keen to 'oblige'.

3.    On the rare occasions when an offender had been considered unsuitable for the work, such as where an offender was 'lazy', CS had removed the offender from the placement and resolved any problems that might have arisen. Some respondents noted the role of the supervisor; for example, 'Having seen them at work and the results, I felt the overseer had slotted them into the jobs he knew they could handle.'

4.    Those offenders that CS staff considered to be untrustworthy or unpredictable were not generally given agency placements. The inspection team noted that CS staff took great care to ensure that recipients were not at risk from the offenders on placement. The only exception was one case in **Aberdeenshire** where an offender had been inappropriately placed and posed a risk to the recipient of the service. **We believe that there are still some lessons which Aberdeenshire can learn from the incident to reduce the likelihood of a re-occurrence.**

5.    The preparations for agency placements were thorough in all three areas and there was a high degree of support for agency staff working directly with offenders following the allocation of an offender. For example 'As their tutor/organiser, I would set up an initial meeting with the Community Service Worker and the offender. This would take place during the course of the club (for adults with learning disabilities). Following a six week settling in period, a special meeting would then take place. Feed back would be ongoing

during this time. Very important between tutor and offender. Offenders are continually interacting with other tutors and helpers to carry out the tasks required'.

6.     For those in a task group, the work was generally of a manual nature involving a minimum degree of skill. Some projects offered greater scope for skills development than others, perhaps through the use of machinery or some recipient contact. All the offenders were able to undertake the tasks allotted to them but needed different levels of instruction, tuition and support. We commend the 'painting room' in Banff to other areas. It allows painting and decorating skills to be learned before application on people's homes and allows for more complex work as skills develop (for example papering with patterned wall paper). **Dundee** told us that they thought The Scottish Office prohibited schemes from providing training for offenders in this way. Whilst CS should not provide employment training for offenders, there is no prohibition against training for CS work. It is unfair to recipients and to offenders that offenders learn essential skills on the job. Each scheme should have the capacity to help offenders learn essential skills needed to meet work standards.

7.     We endorse the use of a workshop environment for assessment and holding difficult to place offenders but this is not enough to justify its use and is not cost effective. We are attracted to the notion of workshops also being seen as service units for a range of projects such as painting and decorating and environmental projects. Both Aberdeenshire and Dundee are already using their workshops to provide a range of products to enhance the quality of their environmental schemes, e.g. fences and picnic tables, seed boxes and refuse bins. Falkirk is considering the development of a workshop. We welcome this and think there is much to learn from the inspection findings and the experience of other areas.

8.     The number of offenders on each task group varied but in each area it was considerably less than were called to attend. The task groups generally consisted of 2 to 4 offenders with 5 being viewed by CS staff as the ideal. The average size of task group during the inspection was 3 in **Dundee**, 4 in **Falkirk** and 2.5 in **Aberdeenshire**. We were told the low offender/supervisor ratio in Dundee was because of the early return to work of a supervisor who had been on sick leave whilst temporary cover was still in place. However in all three areas the supervisors indicated that the ratio was fairly normal. The small size of work group is not efficient or economic. Small work groups are right in some circumstances. Offenders with very poor skills may require a lot of help in a small group or there may be groups of women who are small in number. In order to cater for all offenders and the different challenges they pose for the organisation of CS, it is important to maximise the size of the work groups where this is achievable. **All areas need to find ways to increase the actual size of the task group to the highest number allowed by the type of project and characteristics of the workforce.**

9.     **Dundee** and **Falkirk** both have systems that can monitor the level of attendance and it is an issue that receives regular attention by the CS managers. In **Aberdeenshire** we were concerned to note that such systems were not in place and retrieving the information to assess performance would be difficult and time consuming. In addition, supervisors and managers offered different views of the number of offenders that they expect to attend for a day's work. **CS managers in Aberdeenshire should seek to obtain more accurate and timely information to assist in the efficient management of the service.**

# Chapter 5

# Health and Safety

1.    CS placements must meet current UK and European Health and Safety legislation which includes the requirement to assess each project for Health and Safety risks. On task groups:-

- all the offenders were clear about the work, behaviour and Health and Safety standards required of them;

- all the task group projects in all the areas were supervised in a safe manner at the time of the inspection;

- the supervisors seemed knowledgeable and able in Health and Safety matters;

- all supervisors had First Aid certificates (bar one new staff member in **Dundee** who was due to be trained shortly);

- many supervisors had considerable experience of Health and Safety issues across a range of work environments.

2.    For those on individual agency placements, the responsibility for Health and Safety lay with the agency on the advice of the CS staff. In **Dundee** and **Aberdeenshire** the agency representatives were clear that Health and Safety issues had been addressed with them. In **Falkirk** it does not appear to have been and one inspector observed an offender painting with a loose electric wire crossing her at neck level.  In **Aberdeenshire** we were told that offenders travel on the crew bus in greater numbers than the insurance cover allows.  This has been attended to since the inspection.

3.    Health and Safety requirements are growing and becoming more complex and recent training provided by SWSG has highlighted the importance of this issue.  All three areas were aware that their procedures may need reviewing.  Both **Dundee** and **Falkirk** have properly recorded Health and Safety assessment systems in respect of all tasks.  In **Falkirk** it is part of the general task assessment and the system has considerable merit. **Falkirk** also has a helpful Health and Safety leaflet for offenders on CS which the inspection team commends. In **Aberdeenshire**, only one of the three divisions undertakes a properly recorded Health and Safety risk assessment. Considerable work is needed to bring practice across the whole area up to an acceptable standard. **Aberdeenshire should undertake and record Health and Safety assessments on every placement.**

4.    **Falkirk** has an impressive Health and Safety manual that includes all the advice needed to run a CS scheme.  Supervisors must take 3 sections from the guide with them to placements and consideration is being given to amending the guide for easier site use. **Dundee** has a supervisor's guide that is brief, accessible and transportable.

5.    **The standard of the workshop in Dundee was inadequate and must be improved to reach an acceptable Health and Safety standard.** The rest area was dirty; the workshop area

was cramped and very cold, particularly as the work did not need a great deal of physical energy. We have been told by CS staff at **Dundee** that they have cleaned the rest room, will provide more electrical points for electric tools and are seeking longer term improvements to the workshop. We recognise that improvements may cost a substantial amount of money given the nature of the building. **Falkirk** does not have a workshop. **Aberdeenshire** has two. We saw only one (which was not in operation at the time). It was well kept, had suitable wall mounted gas heaters, the rest area was clean and generally seemed a healthy place to work.

6.　Whilst across the three areas, some offenders were working in warm, comfortable surroundings, most of the offenders were working in cold and sometimes wet and miserable conditions. In Falkirk managers told us that work groups undertake painting and decorating and environmental work through out the year, but during the inspection period all the work was environmental. It took place outside in extremely cold and wet weather. There is a local rule where offenders who do not bring their own lunch must go without (although at each task group site visited this rule was not observed). It is to the credit of the supervisors that they were able to motivate offenders all day in these conditions and we were impressed with the quality of their work. Work continued during all but the worst of weather in which case offenders could not complete their hours for the day as no other work was available. **Falkirk should develop projects that are suitable for work in very bad weather to ensure that working hours can be completed as planned.** A workshop may meet this need.

7.　In all 3 areas many of the offenders we spoke to had not eaten before the start of the day's work and would not be eating until the end of the day, if at all. Lack of food coupled with the conditions in which some of the offenders were working posed Health and Safety risks. Offenders are told to bring food with them but many either cannot afford to do so or do not manage their income well enough to do so. **This issue needs greater attention in the induction process (and assistance given to offenders to plan to have sufficient money for food on placement days if necessary).** CS staff should consider providing hot drinks in the winter.

8.　For Health and Safety reasons or the protection of their own clothing, offenders must wear protective clothing on many projects. Overalls are issued to all offenders working on dirty jobs and should be worn on site. The Scottish Office circular (SWSG 12/96) 'Community Service by Offenders: Public Awareness, Environmental Work and Hours' states that 'authorities should ensure that the clothing is clearly and visibly marked with the wording "Community Service Scheme".'

9.　Whilst protective clothing is needed for Health and Safety reasons, the requirement for clothing to be clearly marked is 'to ensure that community service is visible and the projects carried out known in the local community'. A number of offenders whom we saw working on projects in public areas covered the markings by wearing jackets over them or by rolling the top half of the overalls down. Offenders told us that they found the requirement to wear visible clothing humiliating and some offenders indicated that if forced to display the CS label in public places they would not undertake CS. Supervisors were concerned that the issue could undermine the good order and discipline of the projects. Anonymity in an area is a key feature of the safe and orderly completion of projects. Offenders may otherwise be (and have been) the subject of unwarranted attention by local people keen to cause problems. Outwith the inspection other views that the requirement is welcomed have also been expressed.

## Chapter 6

# Benefit to the community

1.     All of the projects we saw benefited the community.  The beneficiaries gained unpaid labour. Most individual beneficiaries were needy or elderly and could not afford to pay for the work privately. It was unlikely that the work would have been done had CS not been available, although some agencies would probably have used volunteer labour. We found no examples of offenders undertaking work that would otherwise have been done by a paid worker.

2.     In some cases the CS beneficiary was readily identifiable; for example, an elderly person in a day centre.  In other cases the beneficiary was the wider community; for example, clearing a beach.  The offenders expressed strong views about who they considered to be 'deserving' recipients and these were generally elderly people, those with disabilities or those who were poor. Ensuring that they knew who was benefiting from the work and helping them understand how their work benefited the community in its widest sense was a key task for the supervisors.

3.     **We think all three areas should do more to assist the offenders in gaining a better understanding the reparative nature of the CSO.** They need to understand how the completion of unpaid work makes reparation to society for the offence committed, who benefits from the work undertaken, how they benefit and why it is worth doing. Many offenders will spend their time on CS working in task groups with no contact with those who benefit from their work. They may be undertaking environmental work that benefits a community other than their own. Those offenders most likely to work in task groups are likely to be those least able to understand the notion of a beneficiary when not working directly with one. The most able offenders are those most likely to be placed in agencies with direct recipient contact. **More needs to be done at the induction stage of the order to explain to offenders the benefit to the community of the work undertaken.**

4.     The work of CS benefits the community through unpaid labour. Several of the beneficiaries also indicated that there were other, less tangible benefits that were important. Many of the offenders work alongside deprived or disabled members of the community. This increases their awareness of the problems others face and provides opportunities for them to reflect on their own behaviour and lives.  Agency workers told us that the agency clients also benefit from having contact with offenders who they are able to relate to as 'human beings' who act responsibly when given an opportunity to do so.

5.     Many of the questionnaire respondents and all of the agency representatives interviewed, indicated that, by treating offenders as responsible members of the community, they were able to attain the high standards of work and behaviour that was evident across all three schemes.  The agency workers only told their colleagues or clients of the 'volunteer' being an offender on a 'need to know' basis and their treatment of them was indistinguishable from the voluntary or paid helpers.

## Chapter 7

# Equity

**Women Offenders**

1.    Given the high social and economic costs of women with dependants being sentenced to imprisonment it is important that CS schemes provide a suitable alternative for the courts. Overall more women are considered to be unsuitable for CS as a proportion of those referred. Our findings showed that in **Falkirk** a significantly disproportionate number of women referred were considered unsuitable for CS by report writers and one of the sheriffs indicated that CS may also be unsuitable for single parents (invariably women). There were no placements that cater specifically for women which meant that they might have to work in all male work groups. From information contained in the files and discussions with staff we concluded that **the needs of women offenders were not fully considered and there were insufficient placements that properly cater for them.**

2.    We think that the arrangements for the supervision of women offenders on CS are adequate in **Dundee** and **Aberdeenshire**. **Aberdeenshire's** high number of individual placements means that offenders are catered for individually and, where there are special needs, these can be met. **Dundee** tries not to place women alone in work groups of men although this did occur during the inspection. **There is an all female workshop group. We commend this development which may be suitable for replication elsewhere.**

**Health Problems**

3.    Many offenders on CS suffer ill health. Some have insufficient resources to improve diet or leisure habits.  Mental health problems, particularly depression, are very common and a number of offenders have disabilities.  Chronic ill health did not preclude the successful completion of CS and 20 out of the 37 successful completion case files showed incidents of ill health, some serious. At the same time, the orders on some offenders with health problems were being reviewed at court, frequently resulting in the orders being discharged.

4.    It was beyond the scope of the inspection to explore in detail the characteristics of the offenders or the CS schemes that led to successful completion where there were health problems. However we observed some good practice that may have wider application. In **Dundee,** where ill health  seemed particularly  significant, there is a 'light duties' task group which means that CS can be offered to the courts for those with health problems.  In **Aberdeenshire,** one team, through negotiation with local GPs, has improved procedures for dealing with sickness as it arises during the order.  The system discourages offenders from getting sick notes as an 'excuse' for an absence for some other reason and has led to a reduction in absences attributed to sickness.  In **Falkirk** absences are chased up in person on the morning of the failure to attend: **Dundee** is also planning to adopt this system.  Where services are able to provide suitable work for offenders with health problems **coupled** with a

system of enforcing orders that discourage using ill health as a pretext for avoiding doing the work, CS can offer a credible sentence to the courts for those in poor health. **We commend the development of a light duties team in Dundee and the practice adopted in one area in Aberdeenshire of working with GPs to reduce absenteeism attributed to sickness. These measures should have wider dissemination.**

## Ethnic Minorities

5.    Very few ethnic minority offenders are on CS, the maximum being 2 in **Dundee** during the inspection. In **Dundee** there is a new placement working for the local mosque and two of the agency placements the inspectors visited had employees who were very well informed on race issues. All the supervisors in all 3 areas explicitly stated to offenders that racist and sexist behaviour was unacceptable.

## Young Offenders

6.    In **Falkirk** a disproportionate number of young offenders breached their orders. In a random sample in terms of age, 8 of the 9 breaches were of offenders under 25 years of age (compared to 5 out of 8 in **Dundee** and 2 out of 9 in **Aberdeenshire**). Staff in **Falkirk** indicated that provision does not meet the needs of all groups of offenders including young offenders.

7.    **Findings relating to the narrow range of placements available in Falkirk, suggest that a wider review of placements and their suitability for all offenders should be undertaken. Falkirk should develop projects that are suitable for women offenders, those in poor health, those with dependants and young offenders.**

8.    **All authorities in Scotland should review their CS placements and ensure that there is a sufficient range to suit all offenders. Courts should not be precluded from making a CSO for reasons of sex, disability, race, employment or caring for dependants.**

## Firm and Fair Treatment

9.    All the offenders thought their supervisors were firm but fair. The supervisors drew attention to a small group of offenders 'with attitude' who seemed determined at the outset to make life difficult for everybody else. The supervisors had no illusions about the problems created by this small group. They made a point of identifying them quickly - 'you've got to spot these guys early' 'face them with their obligations fair and square' and giving a lot of attention to 'bringing them on'. The supervisors were confident about their ability to engage many of these offenders. They stressed the importance of the supervising officer in enforcing standards where needed.

10.   Whilst there is some good practice in **Aberdeenshire**, we noted that some practices such as the liaison with GPs and the Health and Safety assessments were inconsistently applied. Offenders in **Aberdeenshire** experienced CS differently depending on who their social worker was, as each social worker was able to develop their own CS practices. Some diversity may be appropriate in response to local circumstances, but managers had insufficient knowledge about variable practices. Since the inspection and in order to improve the situation, **Aberdeenshire** have decided to give lead responsibility for CS to a

staff member in the North and also in the South when this part of the scheme is transferred. The aims are to ensure consistency of practice and to develop good practice. Additionally **Aberdeenshire** are using team meetings to develop and spread good practice through out the area and team meeting minutes are now copied across the authority. We welcome these developments. **Aberdeenshire should continue to develop and review recently introduced systems to ensure good practice throughout the area and managers should make themselves more aware of both good and bad practice.**

# Chapter 8

# Effectiveness

1. Successful completion of orders and a reduction in re-offending are significant measures of effectiveness and we considered the contribution the placements might make to this. We were looking for placements that offered the offender a positive experience of CS as a penalty for the harm caused by offending. Two of the areas, **Dundee** and **Aberdeenshire** have started surveying offenders who have completed their CS orders. The **Aberdeenshire** survey is about to be issued. **Dundee** have analysed the first responses from the survey and the findings will inform future practice. Fourteen offenders in **Dundee** have responded to date and all of them thought the work they had undertaken was of benefit to the community and 13 indicated that CS reduced their offending. Few of the offenders interviewed by the inspection team expected that the CSO would reduce offending although some mentioned that a custodial sentence was likely to make it worse. Those that we interviewed were in the middle or early stages of the order and it may take time for offenders to achieve a more accurate assessment of its impact on their attitudes and behaviour. Elsewhere in the report we also note that few offenders understood, at the outset of the sentence, the reparative nature of the sentence or the importance of working, unpaid, for the benefit of others. This is an area that needs to be covered more fully in the induction process.

2. We were impressed with the supervisors in all 3 areas. The supervisors all managed the work and the offenders differently in ways that were right for the supervisor and the task. The majority of supervisors were highly skilled at motivating offenders, setting suitably high standards of work and behaviour and holding the offenders to task. **The characteristics of these supervisors were**

- they worked alongside the offenders in whatever they were doing;

- they demonstrated how tasks needed to be done;

- they supported the offenders in their efforts;

- they helped them to improve their skills;

- they made the experience a learning one as far as the task allowed;

- they took account of the varying abilities.

3. Modelling and example are key attributes of a good supervisor. One beneficiary commented 'Given that these people were new to this area of work and way of doing things, and that they were "forced" into doing it, I think they did well. Much credit to A. and his mate, as leaders, they were very aware of the duties and tasks undertaken and did their best, often in their own time, to ensure the work was completed to a high standard'.

4.    The agency supervisors were extremely committed to the client group they were serving and transmitted this commitment to the offenders. They treated the offenders as volunteers and offenders were primarily motivated by the value of the work. Offenders generally responded well to the high expectations of the agency supervisors.

5.    The painting and decorating of old people's or disabled people's homes provides one of the best experiences of offender/recipient contact. It is in a supervised setting, and with a beneficiary group that the offenders view as 'deserving' and worthwhile. These placements therefore have the potential to have the greatest impact. Whilst we endorse these sort of projects we recognise that there are a number of problems with them. The number of offenders that can work in a small house is limited; supervision has to be very close and care needs to be taken in choosing suitable offenders. Where offenders are placed on projects with little or no direct contact with the beneficiary, it is important that the supervisors explain to them the value of the work and tell them when the work is appreciated.

6.    Individual placements supervised unpaid by an agency are not necessarily cheaper than those supervised by CS staff. Although the agency supervises the offenders, the support by CS staff can be considerable and the placements need a great deal of preparation. We were impressed however with 2 placements that offered considerable value for money whilst achieving all the benefits expected from an individual placement. In **Dundee** there are a number of individual placements at the local zoo where offenders are paired with a staff member for the day. In **Falkirk** a scheme for teaching adults with learning difficulties reading, writing and arithmetic took up to five offenders at any one time.

7.    **Aberdeenshire** has more individual placements (about 50%) due to the demographic nature of the area and we consider this is appropriate. We welcome their current plans for more environmental work but this may be difficult to achieve. There may be insufficient offenders available in any one area to form a work group of an economic size. **Dundee** has a wide range of placements that allow for individual contact if the offender is suitable and individual placements are viewed as a progression through the order. Agency placements account for about 20% of placements and, given the nature of the offender profile, we think this is a proper balance. In **Falkirk** at the time of the inspection almost all of the work undertaken by CS was of a manual nature on environmental projects in task groups. Future work will include more environmental projects and some painting and decorating schemes that may involve recipient contact. The policy of the council is that it supports the development of large scale environmental projects, but not at the expense of individual beneficiaries in the local community, particularly elderly and disabled people. This policy is not being achieved at present and less than 10% of placements have any direct beneficiary contact. **There is scope for more placements with direct beneficiary contact.**

8.    Although further offending may relate to a number of factors, it is important to identify those characteristics of CS that might reduce the risk of re-offending and contribute to successful completion of orders. Gill McIvor's research provides a useful starting point. **National Objectives and Standards for CS should be amended to reflect accurately the impact CS can and should seek to make on the attitudes and behaviour of offenders.**

# Chapter 9

# Summary, Conclusions and Recommendations

## Summary and Conclusions

1.    Community Service is a complex activity. As a sentence of the court it has to meet the requirements of the law and have the confidence of sentencers. It must be credible as a sanction with the community, offenders and recipients. It must be economic whilst providing work for a number of offenders who have never or hardly ever worked, may be in poor health and often lead ill disciplined lives. The work must be completed to a high standard regardless of the skills of those undertaking it and must challenge the capacity of the offender. Swift disciplinary action must be taken where standards of conduct or work are not met and this must be administered fairly. In addition, we agree with the sheriffs in all 3 areas that CS should contribute to preventing further offending. To achieve all of this is a difficult task and requires a high level of management skill and supervision.

## Dundee

2.    The **Dundee** scheme is able to cater for most of the offenders who come before the courts and suitable placements are provided reflecting different characteristics and abilities. There is a wide range of projects available, both agency and group, which provide a range of challenges and opportunities for skills' development. Supervision of offenders is of a high standard and the supervisory staff are of good quality. It is a good scheme.

3.    The workshop is not wholly successful but we have no doubt about its potential. We note that staff are alert to these issues and are examining options for dealing with them. If properly used, the workshop can exploit the opportunities outlined in Chapter 4, Paragraph 7.

4.    Dundee Council believes CS can make a contribution to community safety through its links with community organisations and the creation of a social environment that is less conducive to crime. For example the work undertaken with homeless people and estate improvements can help to reduce crime further. This policy encourages the development of a wide range of imaginative projects and increases the scope for benefiting the wider community alongside benefiting individual recipients.

5.    Sheriffs have considerable confidence in the CS scheme and CS staff ensure they are well informed about the work.

## Aberdeenshire

6.    In **Aberdeenshire** the range of projects is limited, reflecting the low numbers of offenders on CS at any one time in each locality. They are suitable, provide for a range of skills and offer challenges to the offender. The flexible work arrangements for those coming

off fishing boats or temporary employment are right in the circumstances. They allow some offenders to undertake CS and get through their orders who would otherwise be denied the opportunity. The workshop in Banff provides opportunities for a range of work experience, under close supervision if needed, and skills development before starting work in people's homes.

7. Managers were not as well informed as they should be about key aspects of practice, good and bad, in different locations and consequently significant events/practices were not properly reviewed by managers and lessons learned. We appreciate that this may be due in part to the characteristics of the area. However, we also found that managers do not have ready access to up to date information partly because the information systems on which they rely are inadequate: to improve on this may need expenditure. Notwithstanding these factors (geography, technology and costs) management also needs to improve the quality of its contact with staff and engage more actively with them in reviewing and developing practice.

8. Local CS practices have developed (for example Health and Safety and project assessments) but we saw no consistent area wide approach to developing good practice. We are pleased to note that the service is now introducing measures to remedy this, including a lead officer and greater sharing of information.

9. Health and Safety assessments of projects were not undertaken in every case and offenders travelling on service vehicles were not always covered by insurance. These matters have been attended to since the inspection.

10. The CS supervisors were impressive in their commitment to beneficiaries and offenders and were the real strength of the scheme. However management needs to do further work on developing a sense of common purpose for the scheme if supervisors are to have the support they need to get the most out of offenders.

**Falkirk**

11. In **Falkirk** there were a number of useful management information systems in place and the processes for ensuring progress though orders were impressive. We also found some good placements; for example, a project for people with learning difficulties. The standard of supervision was consistently good.

12. **Falkirk** has developed mainly task group placements and at the time of the inspection these were all of an environmental, manual nature. The shift in emphasis meets the requirements of unpaid work and approximates most closely to recent government instructions that the work should be sufficiently physically demanding with a greater emphasis on environmental work. On the other hand, the small range of projects in operation is not meeting the needs of the court or the local authority's own priorities for CS placements. The authority wants CS also to benefit individuals in the community who are elderly or disabled who would not otherwise be able to receive a service. What makes **Falkirk** different from the other schemes is the lack of variety and the lack of opportunity for offenders to develop a range of skills or progress beyond task group work. There is little direct contact with the beneficiary. The purpose of CS and how it benefits the community is not explained to the offenders and some offenders do not view the work as 'worthwhile'.

13   The needs of women offenders and those with special needs were not well understood and did not attract enough attention. We were also concerned that those offenders who could not cope with the demands of the task group were viewed as unsuitable for CS.

14.   The **Falkirk** scheme is missing opportunities to improve quality. We agree with one sheriff's view that the first step is to increase the range of placements. This would allow the court to use CS more extensively, allow the community to benefit in more ways, provide for a wider range of offenders and increase the opportunities for offenders to learn new skills.

15.   We are pleased that **Falkirk** is actively considering the development of a workshop, especially as there was no task group work available, under cover, during particularly bad winter weather.  Management may see merit in CS staff visiting other schemes to find examples of projects for possible replication in **Falkirk.**

### All 3 areas

16.   The quality of supervisors across the three schemes was impressive. They used a wide range of skills to motivate offenders and to achieve high standards of work and placement behaviour. They provided excellent role models for (mostly) male offenders. Where possible, they extended the skills of offenders and matched their skills to the task.

17.   The work of CS is of benefit to the community, is valued by those who benefit directly from the work, is of a high standard and the behaviour of offenders whilst on placements is good.

18.    Some of the examples of good practice which we found, such as the light duties team and the female offender task group in **Dundee** and work with GPs to reduce sickness absence in **Aberdeenshire** deserve to be considered for replication elsewhere.

19.   There is scope for greater efficiency in the size of the work groups. This is particularly important, if more offenders who might need greater supervision or smaller work groups are to be catered for,

20.    In all three schemes there is scope for improving the induction processes.  Health and Safety is covered with varying degrees of comprehensiveness.  The standards of behaviour and the conditions of CS are covered well in all 3 areas. The benefit to the community or the reparative nature of CS is not covered systematically in any of the areas. A fuller explanation of the work undertaken by CS, the skills required and the opportunities that may be available for progression depending on reliability, learning, etc. would also enhance the schemes. Following the inspection supervisors in Falkirk have introduced an explanation of the purpose of the work and who benefits at the start of each day's work. We commend this development. **We recommend that there is an induction programme developed for all offenders undertaken either individually or in  groups that covers the following**

- **the purpose of the sentence and how the offender 'makes good' the harm done by his or her offence through unpaid work**

- **Health and Safety (including bringing food when undertaking physically demanding work)**

- **standards of behaviour and work**

- requirements of the order

- the skills to be acquired, used and improved on the placement

- benefit to the community

21.    The inspection team had not intended that the government circular requiring marked clothing and vehicles would be the focus for this inspection. Concerns about aspects of its implementation were, however, drawn to our attention on many occasions and in all 3 areas. As this was not a significant element of the planned inspection, we did not test out our findings in a systematic way. Nevertheless, we have concerns about some aspects of the circular.

22.    The government circular states that "much more needs to be done to ensure that community service is visible and the projects carried out known in the local community." Local authorities were required to take on Local Publicity, Identification of Projects, Markings on Vehicles and Protective Clothing. (See Appendix attached).

23.    One aspect of the current requirement to publicise CS, through the wearing of visible clothing and marked vehicles, has consequences not intended by its introduction. Some offenders find it humiliating and some supervisors fear that it undermines good discipline and de-motivates offenders.  **We recommend that The Scottish Office reviews this aspect of the circular.**

24.    Oddly  the prevention of re-offending is not currently an objective of CS. It is however a primary aim of sentencers and those organising and managing CS. Research indicates that it can make a contribution. Offenders and sentencers also think that it can help reduce offending. The development of work discipline, skills and self-respect all contribute to this objective as do many other factors. **We recommend that National Objectives and Standards for CS should be amended to reflect the impact CS can and should seek to make on the attitudes and behaviour of offenders.**

# List of Recommendations

**Dundee**

1.   To improve its potential as a workshop, we recommend that Dundee Council undertakes a review of the muster and dispersal arrangements at the beginning and the end of the day and the workshop is improved to reach an acceptable Health and Safety standard. (Chapter 3, Paragraph 17; Chapter 5, Paragraph 5.)

**Aberdeenshire**

2.   The Council should consider the safeguards needed to ensure that offenders do not pose a risk to recipients of CS. (Chapter 4, Paragraph 4)

3.   The Council should ensure that Health and Safety assessments are undertaken in respect of every placement. (Chapter 5 Paragraph 3)

4.   Managers should make themselves more aware of both good and bad practice. We recommend that Aberdeenshire continues to develop and review recently introduced systems that ensure good practice is disseminated through out the authority. (Chapter 7, Paragraph 10)

5.   CS managers in Aberdeenshire should seek to obtain more accurate and timely information to assist in the efficient management of the service. (Chapter 4, Paragraph 9).

**Falkirk**

6.   Falkirk Council should increase its range of placements in consultation with the sheriffs so that those offenders the courts might wish to sentence to CS can be placed. (Chapter 3 Paragraph 9)

7.   Falkirk Council should develop projects that are suitable for women offenders, those in poor health, those with dependants and young offenders. (Chapter 7, Paragraphs 1 & 7)

8.   Arrangements and projects need to be in place to ensure that all offenders placed on CS are working within 21 days of sentence as required by National Standards. (Chapter 3, Paragraph 10)

9.   Falkirk council should ensure that placements are sufficiently challenging; provide opportunities for recipient contact; utilise offenders skills and that there is work under cover for the worst of winter weather. (Chapter 3, Paragraph 22; Chapter 5, Paragraph 6; Chapter 8, Paragraph 7.)

**Nationally**

10.   We commend the development of a light duties team and a women's teams in **Dundee** and the practice adopted in one team in **Aberdeenshire** of working with GPs to reduce

absenteeism through sickness. **Dundee** and **Aberdeenshire** should review how these developments are working and provide an account for wider dissemination.(Chapter 7, Paragraphs 2 & 4)

11.   All councils should review their CS placements and ensure that there is a sufficient range so that courts are not precluded from making a CSO for reasons of sex, disability, race, employment or caring for dependants. (Chapter 7, paragraph 8.)

12.   We recommend that areas consider the characteristics of good placement supervisors. (Chapter 8, Paragraph 2.) To ensure future recruitment of high quality of CS supervisors, these characteristics should become part of the selection criteria for CS supervisors.

13.   All councils should find ways to increase the actual size of the task group. (Chapter 4, Paragraph 8.)

14.   We recommend that all councils review their induction process to ensure that the areas listed below are included. SWSG should commission the development of a 'tool kit' for use with all offenders either individually or in  groups which covers the following

- the purpose of the sentence and how the offender 'makes good' the harm done by his or her offence through unpaid work

- Health and Safety (including bringing food when undertaking physically demanding work)

- standards of behaviour and work

- requirements of the order

- the skills to be acquired, used and improved on the placement

- benefit to the community

(Chapter 5, Paragraph 7; Chapter 6, Paragraph 3; Chapter 9, Paragraph 20.)

### The Scottish Office

15.   We recommend that the requirement to wear marked clothing is reviewed. (Chapter 9, Paragraph 23.)

16.   We recommend that National Objectives and Standards are amended to allow supervisors to supervise more than five offenders in a work group where appropriate. (Chapter 4, Paragraph 8)

17.   We recommend that National Objectives and Standards for CS should be amended to accurately reflect the impact CS can and should seek to make on the attitudes and behaviour of offenders.
(Chapter 8, Paragraph 8.)

# APPENDIX

**Extract from Government Circular SWSG12/96**

**Identification of Schemes and Improved Publicity**

The Government believes that much more needs to be done to ensure that community service is visible and the projects carried out known in the local community. Local authorities should therefore take the following **action** to achieve these objectives:

### Local Publicity.

Authorities should seek every opportunity to publicise the benefits produced by community service schemes in the local media.

### Identification of Projects

Wherever appropriate, authorities should arrange for the identification of projects by means of signs showing that the work is being or has been carried out by a community service scheme.

### Markings on Vehicles

Authorities should arrange for vehicles used by community service schemes to be marked to indicate this. Such markings may be permanent or temporary.

### Protective Clothing

Authorities are already required to provide suitable protective clothing. Where protective clothing is worn at a placement, for health and safety reasons or to protect participants' own clothing, authorities should ensure that the clothing is clearly and visibly marked with the wording "Community Service Scheme". (Existing stocks of protective clothing should be adapted where possible.) The requirement to wear this protective clothing when participating in relevant work should be regarded as a normal reasonable requirement of supervision. The test of whether protective clothing is reasonably required is where protection would be worn whether or not the person was a participant in a community service scheme, and where a claim for compensation might result in the event of protective clothing not being provided. The same protective clothing should be worn by all participants in the community service project, including supervisory staff. Only in exceptional circumstances (for instance where the offender is placed with an organisation which has its own arrangements or requirements for protective clothing) will this not apply.

Printed by The Stationery Office 6/97 (160744)